Words of Appreciation

ZENDOODLE COLORSCAPES: WORDS OF APPRECIATION.
Copyright © 2021 by St. Martin's Press. All rights reserved.
Printed in Canada. For information, address
St. Martin's Press, 120 Broadway, New York, NY 10271.

www.castlepointbooks.com

The Castle Point Books trademark is owned by Castle Point Publishing, LLC.
Castle Point books are published and distributed by St. Martin's Publishing Group.

ISBN 978-1-250-27539-4 (trade paperback)

Our books may be purchased in bulk for promotional, educational, or business use.
Please contact your local bookseller or the Macmillan Corporate and Premium
Sales Department at 1-800-221-7945, extension 5442, or by email
at MacmillanSpecialMarkets@macmillan.com.

First Edition: 2021

10 9 8 7 6 5 4 3 2 1

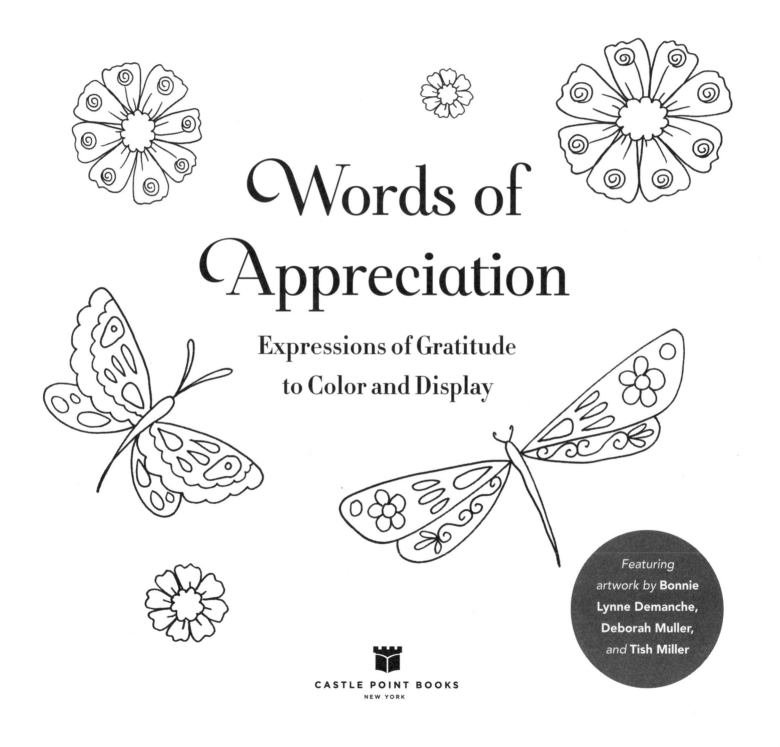

zendoodle colorscapes

Words of Appreciation

Expressions of Gratitude to Color and Display

Featuring artwork by **Bonnie Lynne Demanche, Deborah Muller,** *and* **Tish Miller**

CASTLE POINT BOOKS
NEW YORK

Always remember
You are braver
than you believe,
Stronger than you seem,
And smarter
than you think

e.

I can't help falling in love with you

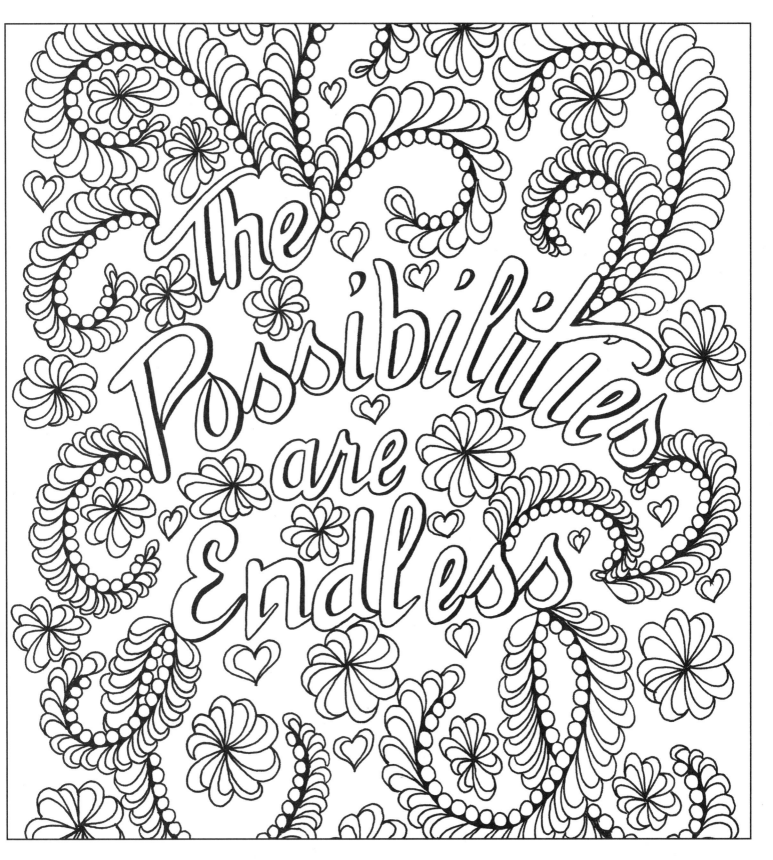

The sound of your voice swims quietly through me

When we are in love, we are open to all that life has to offer

Your VIBE attracts your TRIBE